Infinit

Poetically speaking
The Eyes Don't Lie

By Ovlina Lewis

"Ovi"

outskirts
press

The opinions expressed in this manuscript are solely the opinions of the author and do not represent the opinions or thoughts of the publisher. The author has represented and warranted full ownership and/or legal right to publish all the materials in this book.

Infinite Thoughts
Poetically Speaking, The Eyes don't lie
All Rights Reserved.
Copyright © <2013>Ovlina Lewis

Images © 2012 JupiterImages Corporation. All rights reserved - used with permission.

This book may not be reproduced, transmitted, or stored in whole or in part by any means, including graphic, electronic, or mechanical without the express written consent of the publisher except in the case of brief quotations embodied in critical articles and reviews.

Outskirts Press, Inc.
http://www.outskirtspress.com

ISBN: 978-1483905044

This custom interior poetry template is Copyright © 2012, Outskirts Press, Inc.

PRINTED IN THE UNITED STATES OF AMERICA

Dedicated to

My loving family and every heart I am able reach. Thank you for all the love and support.

Contents of Infinite Thoughts

Chapter 1

Infinite Thoughts of Wisdom

Formal introduction	1
Eye Am Who Eye Am	2
Enchanted Garden	3
Serendipity's Mystery	4
Clarity	5
Chance	6
2	7
Inner Peace	9
Meditation	10
Infinite Thoughts	13
Baggage Be Free	15
A Man's World	17

Chapter 2

Infinite Thoughts of Love

As One	20
Love So	21
Destiny	22
In Too Deep	24
Soul Mates	27
Twin Flames	29
What is Love	30
Love Interpreted	31
With You	33

Down for the Count	35
Sweet Tooth	37
Promise	38
For You	39
Falling in Love with You Again	40
The Letter	41

Chapter 3
Infinite Thoughts of Sensuality

So Damn Good	44
Sensual Play	45
Imagine That	47

Chapter 4
Infinite Thoughts of Pain and Broken Hearts

You Promised	49
Why Must I Cry	50
Invisible Tears	51
Passive Aggressive Heart	53
Painless	56
S.H.A.M.E O.N Y.O.U	57
Disappear	58
I'm leaving	59
Love Was Here	60
You	61
Voicemail... Final Warning	62

Chapter 5
Infinite Thoughts of Motivation and Inspiration

Motivation Equals Determination	66
Sweet Merlot	67
Lost and Found	70
Confident	72
Beautiful Women	73

Chapter 6
Infinite Thoughts Thinking Outside the Box

Beware	76
Propaganda	77
Eye to the Sky	80
Matrix	81

Chapter 7
Infinite Thoughts of Sincere Dedications

My King	85
Mother	88
Creation Within	91
My Child	93
Anxiously Expecting	94
Found	95
Ovlina	97
Family Tree in Concrete	98
Devil in Disguise	101
Last Words	103

Infinite Thoughts of Wisdom

The Formal Introduction

Formally introducing you to the I, the us, the we
All parts combined as a whole to create me
Lives of multiplicity but only one soul
Throughout the journey
Reinventing the superwoman
I personally assembled manually
Adding more badges of honor
As I submerge and re- emerge with new discoveries
Unearthing the beauty of which is the true me
God given abilities inherited distinctively
Combined with my mind and creativity
Understanding my purpose
My power to influence dynamically
Able to see in the dark with clarity
Rich in life through my spirituality
Devoted to help when I can, with sincerity
Controlling the cards that were dealt for me
Fulfil and manifest my own destiny
Then pay it forward charitably
Even if I touch only one heart
Then my job is complete

Eye Am who Eye Am

See me as Eye am
Not for how you portray me
Except the depth of my spirit
Don't try to manipulate or sway me
Embrace my beauty
Encourage my mind
Ask of me what you don't understand
But overstand that Eye am who Eye am
And will not change for any hu-man
Acknowledge my determination
Respect my fight
Never force your values upon me
Heavily overstand that Eye govern and dictate
The decisions of my life

Enchanted Garden

Blindsided by intentions
No caution signs
Only a slippery road
Laced with wild flowers
And daggering vines
Spiraling out of control
Unguarded with freedom to grow
Pondering whether or not to enter
The Enchanted Garden
Or leave well enough alone
Attention diverted to a solitaire black rose
Whose thorns await hidden
Blinded by the sunlight's gold
Seduced in a hypnotic trance
Reaching out with tunnel vision
Pleasure instantly turns to pain
When the thorns emerge
And cut with precision
Breaking the spell
Returning all senses
Purpose and reality revealed
Delusion or fact
Faced with choice
Whether to bandage my wound and move forward
Or capture the moment
Backtrack and never look back

Serendipity's Mystery

I feel you, I sense you from afar
I feel the existence of your spirit
Though I don't know who you are
Maybe we met before, perhaps in my dreams
Or was it a vision that I vividly seen
Precognitive perception of an event
That hasn't begun
Patiently awaiting serendipities outcome
Remaining a mystery in the sub consciousness
Of my mind
Until fate is revealed
One moment in time

Clarity

As I dive into the divine
Of the minds first eye
I go within to understand
What the logical can't comprehend
Interpreting the messages
Most disregard as
Daydreaming hazily
Instead I quiet my mind
Connect spiritually
And listen for clarity

Chance

If by chance, there is a chance
To chance taking a chance
What are the chances
That chance is only chance
Maybe chance isn't a chance after all
Chances are that chance arose do to circumstance
And circumstance provided
A chance to take a chance
Maybe what shall be, shall be if it may
Take a chance
Chances are it was meant to be anyway

2...

2 much 2 ask 2 lend a hand
2 feed and nurture a starving man
2 hear the words of the old and wise
2 bond with child and answer their whys
2 comfort the hearts of the less fortunate in need
2 think of others and less about greed
2 uplift, support and respect thy neighbor
2 encourage, be honest, kindhearted and fair
2 know thyself and not the facade
Is to be at peace with self and 1 with God

Inner peace

A piece of inner peace
Goes a very long way
Tranquility of the mind
Keeps you grounded
Washing negativity away
Harmony and balance
Increases the quality of life
Insight and intuition
Helps you determine wrong from right
The power of love is endless
With boundaries unforeseen
Incorporating all this into one's life
Enables you to accomplish anything

Meditation

I sit in silence, void of the mind
Grounded with earth
A cord to the divine
Cocoon of protection
Engulfed with light
Connected to source
And consciousness of Christ
Aligning the two
True self and vessel
Connecting my spirit
On an universal level
Breathing in love
Exhaling what I release
Aligning my centers
Spinning in sync
Bringing my focus
To my minds first eye
I direct my attention
To see what realty hides
Every thought is a picture
Every picture is a thought
Intuitively I am able
To connect all the dots
Prepared to travel

Through the astral portals of my mind
Alternate planes of existence
Through space with no time
Guided by light
Messengers of Christ
Assisting my journey
Dear guardians of mines
Achieving a state of clarity and balance
By unlocking the gifts
Of my God given talents
Which enable me to see what the matrix is about
Metaphor for a box
That I'll gladly step out
Recording all lessons
As directed I should
Then return from my journey
And apply for my greatest good
Namaste

Infinite Thoughts

Love, patience, balance, WAKE UP, eyes wide shut, programmed, sexuality, emasculation, acceptance, harmony, balance, aggression, peace, mind, body, soul, INFINITE THOUGHTS, heart, growth, change, peace, abandonment, equality, RESPECT, love, passion, regret, passion, live, life, creation, damage, perseverance, peace within, WAKE UP, no pain, no gain, lost, found, poetry, freedom, expression, AmBiTiouZ Mind, INFINITE THOUGHTS, music, poetry,

Honor, longevity, pray, meditate, forgive, let go, believe, trust, educate, teach, learn, laughter, beauty, redefine, THINK OUTSIDE THE BOX, WAKE UP, as above, so below, spirituality, King, Queen, virtue, ignorance, hate, rage, discrimination, revelation, ascension, enlightenment, love, INFINITE THOUGHTS

Baggage be free

Can you dig deep
Can you reach my soul
Can you relinquish and uncover my secrets, desires and fantasies that are buried beneath layers of never ending emotions, pain and fears that were laid by those who walked before you
Can you... Will you... Will you surpass the last that fell short of being victorious in my journey for bliss, happiness and happiness...
Can you see what's behind my eyes
Not just what's visually presented when you look at my body
Distracted by my curves... my flesh... my lips... my thighs
No! But my eyes... because the eyes don't lie...
They tell the story of where you been and where you want to go
They are the gateway to the soul
Both selfish of me and unfortunate for you, the wall still stands

Laid brick by brick by the last man...
The last man responsible for the baggage I now carry
I carry because I'm scared...
Scared that you too will do what most claim not to do...
Break hearts, lie, cheat and deceive...
Keep women, lies, secrets and betrayal up the sleeve
While delivering false hopes and empty promises all while you scheme for the cream of what's between them thighs... them thighs
I want you to want what's behind my eyes... because what's behind my eyes, lies my mind
Once you can unlock that and reach soul...
My heart will follow and maybe then I can let go of those bags that weigh me down... and be free to be free
To love unconditionally both you and me
Without doubt, resistance and hesitance
Love without negligence
Free to be free
To love free...
Live free...
Will you set me free?

A Man's World

You're the man but you really need a girl like me
Hold you down, build you up and keep
You off the streets
Good lovin' I provide and I'm always down to ride
Every king needs a queen right by his side

You're the man and I give you that
You need a real woman who's down
And will have your back
A little crazy time to time
But knows how to act
And when you throw it at me
I can throw it back

You're the owner I'm the captain of the team
We built this empire
I helped to boost your self esteem
Never too dependent
Let you do your own thing

You're the man and I give you that
It takes a woman like me to keep you coming back
You can look but will not find
A better partner or lover
A mean cook and a damn good mother
It's a man's world, but real women make the world go round
If you're fortunate to find one, make sure to lock her down

Infinite Thoughts of Love

As One

We started as seeds

That planted in earth

Then sprouted together

Love coming first

We grew stronger and closer

Blossoming by the day

Seeing your heart as a flower

Delicate in everyway

Appreciating your beauty

As we grow together under the sun

Vowing to be by your side

Till our roots merge as one

Love So...

Love of new
So gentle
Love inflamed with passion
So tantalizing
Love based on the physical
So infatuated
Love without trust
So shallow
Love without boundaries
So fulfilling
Being in love with you
So worth it

Destiny

Last night you made love to my soul
You touched my heart in ways I never knew existed
You caressed every inch of my body without ever
Making a physical connection
You allowed my mind and body to float freely
through ecstasy
While you verbally massaged passion into my heart
When you whispered your words of love in my ear
every Nerve
And sensation was triggered
Excited with the anticipation of your next lyrics of
affection
That's when you did it...
You sealed the moment
Time stood still as you gazed into my eyes and told
me
You loved me without ever parting your lips
I returned the feelings with
A whimper, a sigh, a single tear drop of the eye
I placed your hand on my heart

To let you know that it's yours
It beats only for you
Before I could exhale you wrapped your arms around me
With the tightest yet most gentle grip
And that when we both knew
That our hearts now beat as one
Our souls were intertwined
And that fate now smiled upon us because
We discovered a virgin love so pure
Love everlasting
Love with no boundaries or limitations
The true feelings behind the words "I Do"
A love created and made for just me and you
Love evident of being heaven sent
Love unconditional
Love everlasting
True love
A destiny

In Too Deep

What can be a rainy day for some
May be a parade of sunshine for others
On this one in particular was the day we became lovers
Though we agreed to only become friends
Fate had another plan
Despite the fact that you had a woman and I had a man
Even though we knew it was wrong
It felt sooo, sooo good
To do, want and say things by moral we knew we never should
To allow and accept feelings of love from another
And it not be the type of love you feel for
Friends, possessions or your brother
But the love you feel when your hearts and bodies are on fire
A fire fueled by passion, lust and desire
Tell me, now that it's done
Where do we go from here
How can it not end other than pain, heartache and tears
It's too late to turn back now
Emotions are to strong too just up and walk away
Especially when they are growing stronger by the day

Could the Physical ever be transformed into the emotional
If so what could it become
To want to love but not have love to give
How could we share something we are already committed to
A Relationship
How could we continue to engage in something that should already be sacred
Romance
How can we give or accept something that has already been given away
Our Hearts
I know you want me but...
Do you love me... do you want to love me
If you did would you tell me
If I told you that I loved you
Would you believe me?
Would I believe myself?
Is it even possible to be in love with two people?
And if so.... do you want too?

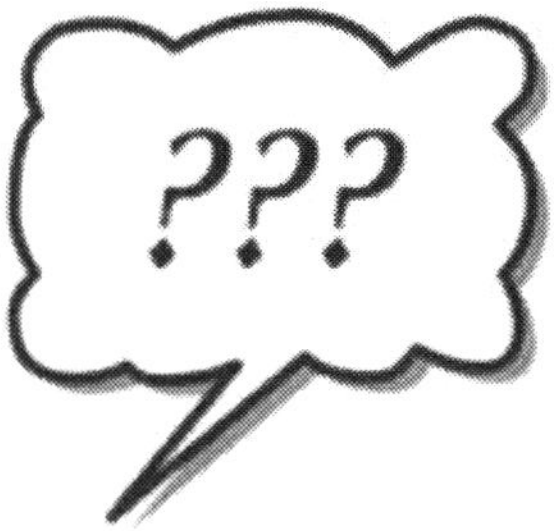

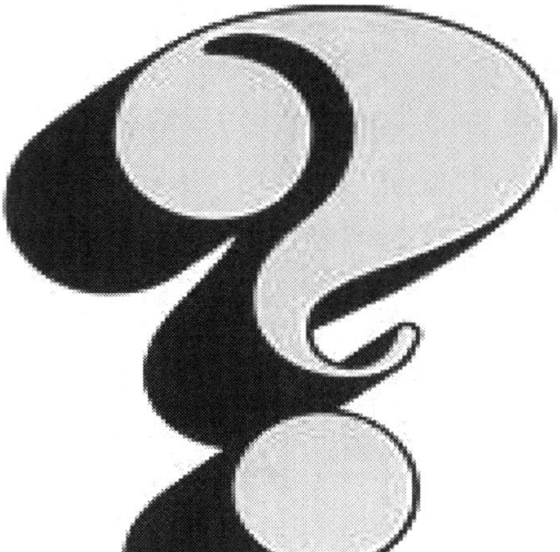

Soul Mates

Day in and day out,
I ask myself are things as real as they seem
Is my heart playing tricks on me
Have I fallen in love
Or am I stuck in a dream
Is it possible the love I yearned for
Has only been footsteps away
Have I been unknowingly starring at the face of my destiny
Each and every day
Then I ask myself if this is real
Why is it that I love him the way that I do
Is it the way that he looks at me
Or the passion in his voice when he says he loves me too
Maybe it's the way he gazes into my eyes
And I can't help but smile
Maybe it's the way he makes me blush
Uncontrollably like a child
Is it that he knows what to say and do

To send me floating on cloud nine
Or the sincerity and confidence when he tells me
I am his and he is mines
Perhaps because we are so much alike
That it sometimes feels like we share the same soul
Maybe because us being together is what our future beholds
All is true, despite how amazing it may seem
I will forever be his queen and he will always reign as my King

Twin Flames

Twin flames
Souls burning with synchronicity
Dancing in harmony
Glow of divinity
Soul energy connection
Intertwined with perfection
Unconditional love and light
Ying and Yang
Day to night
Harmonic balance
Duality merged as one
Flames burning together
Bright as the sun
One as the other
Each as the same
Connected in spirit
The souls of twin flame

What is Love

Can anybody anywhere explain to me about love
I hear it's a wonderful feeling that's sent from above
What is love, can anyone break it down
Can you see it, touch it, does it come with sound
Is love an action or a sense of devotion
Is love a feeling or group of emotions
Is love just a phrase that some couples say
Or is it a predator in the night
Who swallows your heart like its prey
Why don't I know love
Did it somehow pass me by
Until I find it for myself
I'll keep my questions buried inside

Love Interpreted

What is love?
The question constantly boggles my mind
As I search deeper for the answer
I'm finding it harder to find
I believe it to be a wonderful thing that two people share
An overwhelming bundle of emotions
Constantly showing your mate that you care
Don't be mistaken, because you can sometimes be fooled by
Mental and physical stimulation
You might find that the feelings you think are love,
Are mere infatuation
When you love someone you, love them for who they are
All the little things they say and do
Seeing past all flaws and imperfections

Being committed, honest and true
Always respectful of ones thoughts, heart and wishes
Late night conversations, hugs and early morning forehead Kisses
One thing for sure, if you find it in its purest state
Hold on and cherish it
Let it grow deep
Never let it get away

With You

It was a sunny day
The first time I saw you
My clouds went away
My sky turned blue
My heart dropped so fast
I could feel it at my feet
I was left without tone
I couldn't even speak
My body felt weak
My knees began to buckle
I felt sweat run down
My arms to my knuckles
Too shy to talk to you
I thought my words
You would reject and the thought of another heartache
I couldn't accept
Finally I worked up the nerve to talk to you
I was amazed to find
You were feeling me too
So sweet and caring
Special indeed
Realizing with you
Is where I want to be

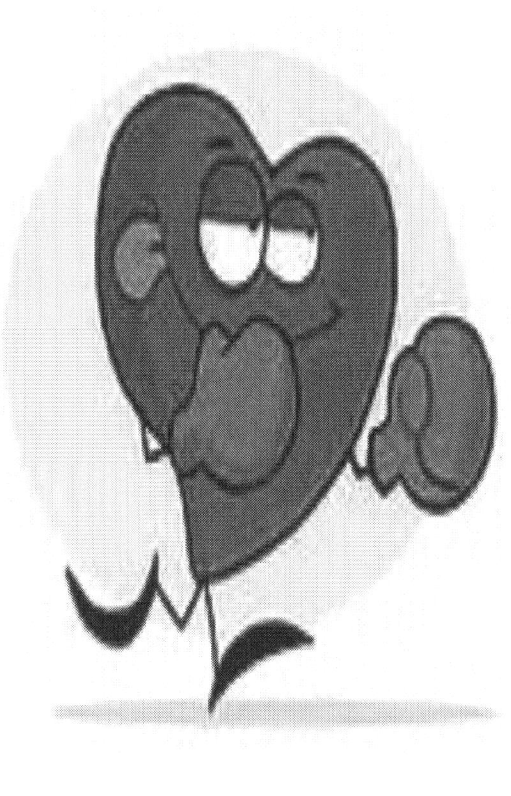

Down for the Count

Greatest fight of my life
When I entered loves ring
There was no need for training
Confident
I was prepared for anything
But as we stood face to face
I knew there was no competition
The beauty in your eyes
Sent my fight into submission
Been in many fights before
But this bout was different
Not the usual competitor
You were in this to win it
The bell rung, and I danced around to feel you out
Tried to study your moves
And see what you were about
Let my guard down once
You managed to step in
You hit me with love
That's when the damage begin
Tried to shake it off
Because my hearts tittle is on the line
But the look on your face said
" prepare to be mines"

Thought to myself
Did I really meet my match
Thought I covered all the basics
Now I can't even react
To the combination you put on me
Got me under attack
Ready to let down my guard
And not even fight back
Dazed in my mind
As I look in your eyes
Why am I even fighting
Is what I realize
No need to resist or continue this bout
Your love has already conquered
And I was down for the count

Sweet Tooth

Almond Joy moments
Chocolate Cherry kisses
Licorice tight hugs
With Bubble Gum wishes
Cotton Candy touch
With a Hot fudge embrace
An Ice Cream love
On a Hot Chocolate day
The Butter to my Pecan
Sweet like Honeydew
The Crunch to my Nestle
You're my Sweet Tooth

Promise

Promise to hold me close
Stay by my side
Comfort me when I need love the most
Promise to never leave
Promise to protect me
Promise to cherish me and respect me
Promise to devote yourself to me, to us
Always love me
Promise

For You

For you I direct all my
Love, kindness and attention
My heart, body and soul
A tremendous amount of affection
For you I try my best
To keep our love hot like fire
Trying to be all the companion you need
And give you what you heart desires
For you and only you
My feelings are sincere and true
Words cannot express all the love I have
For You

Falling in Love with You Again...

Every time I see your face
It's like I'm falling in love again
Every time I'm near you babe
It's like I don't want that moment to end
Because I love you
I place no one before you
You're my everything
Don't ever leave me
Without you I would go insane
Every day with you is like
Falling in love
Falling in love with you again
Being with you feels like
Finding comfort in my best friend
The way you give me love
Is deeper than words comprehend
We found a love so true
Enriched with all the love you bring
A love everlasting
Endures through all the joy and pain
Everything going through is worth
Falling in love with you again

The Letter

    Last night I wrote a letter... it was addressed to you! I never had any intentions on sending it, but I felt I had to address or better yet confess, that this friend stuff isn't working for me! I'm a mess... It's not that I don't want to be your friend... maybe it's because I wanna be more! I wanna be ya girl... ya companion, ya lova'... The silhouette you see at night when you roll over...

    When I'm around you I try to play it cool, knowing I wanna act a damn fool... When I see you with a girl... I think damn that should be me! I should be the one you lust for... the one you adore... Go to the gym for... buy the mag xxl's for... Damn! I want you more and more and more... Every time I see you I get lost with my imagination, trapped by infatuation... but motivated by my determination... to get you... because all I need is one chance... One chance is all it would take, but then I look at what's at stake... and I don't know if I wanna risk it... because if we go there and I confess... get this off my chest... who knows

What would happen… Things would surely change, and why should I risk it, if I don't even know if you feel the same... Or even if you noticed that lately when we're togetha... there's a little extra twist in my hips... more stride in my walk... More gloss on my lips... Do you even sense these feelings exist?
I'm usually not shy when it comes to my feelings or a guy but... you got me twisted, and you don't even know... because in your mind... you're just my homie, my friend, my bro'... and I don't wanna ruin the friendship that's already so strong... but Damn!... In my heart, my life... With me is where you really belong! Till I gather up the courage to tell you the truth or deliver this letter... I must go on like thing's are the same as usual, and try to keep my feelings togetha!

Infinite Thoughts of Sensuality

So Damn Good

Love **So** Good

Passion **So** Deep

Emotions **So** High

Knees **So** Weak

      Damn who See's

      Damn who Knows

      Damn the Place

      Damn these Clothes

           Good Feelings

           Good Sensations

           Good Rhythm

           Good Vibrations

Good and **Deep**, So **High** that I'm **Weak**
See and **Know** the **Places** to go with me and no
Clothes
So you can **Feel** the **Sensations** Of my **Rhythmic**
Vibrations

So Damn Good

Sensual Play

Would you like to play a game?
See I enjoy mental and physical stimulation and I
would love to pick your brain
The game is actually quite simple
Comes with the perk of me doing all the work
A game of ask and tell
Where I ask the questions
And only through body language
Are the answers revealed
There is only one rule to the game
But who cares, rules are meant to be broken
Ready to play?

Do you think you can tame this lioness
My inner beast
Do you think you can quench my licentious thirst
Will you invigorate me
Can you help me release the sweet nectars
Brewing inside
Can you relieve me of the pressure
Barricaded by my thighs
Can you make it hurt in a way that it feels so so good
Can you twist and bend my body
In ways I never knew it could

That was the warm up round

Glad to see I have your full attention
Well enough talking about me
For part two
I'm more interested in finding out more about you
What are your desires
What ignites your flame
Would you like if I lasciviously teased you
Would it drive you insane
Does my aggressive sensuality intimidate you
Do you like that I can take charge
Or would you rather me be tender
Which would make the game hard

Pardon me for the mental intrusion
But we both win in my conclusion
Thus ending the game of my
Projected illusions

Imagine That

I could never have you
Just as you could never have me
For now let's pretend things aren't as bad
As they appear to be
Imagine me as your lady
And you as my man
Imagine it's me you come home too
Imagine that's your ring I wear on my left hand
Imagine being able to hold me, touch me,
Kiss me and caress me
Love me, mold me, freak me, sex me
Unfortunately it is what it is
Mere fantasy far from being reality
It can never be more
We both know in all actuality
However the thought of it sounds nice
But for now I guess the fantasy will have to suffice
Imagine that

Infinite Thoughts of Pain & Broken Hearts

You Promised

You promised to be there for me
You abandoned me
You promised to protect me
You made me the victim
You promised to cherish and honor me
You disrespected me
You promised to be my rock
You walked out and watched me crumble
You promised to always fight for me
You never had my back
You promised to always love me
You broke my heart

Why Must I Cry

Why must I cry
Why must I fill with pain and misery I bury inside
Why do you purposely hurt me for no apparent reasons why
Is it that you like to see me cry
Does it make you feel better inside
Do you find pleasure in watching my heart slowly die
Does the weakness of my emotions fuel your pride
Wouldn't you rather see me smile than agonize
Or because misery love company
You brought me along for the ride
To trample my heart and redden my eyes
Ask why am I hurt then half apologize
Temporary soothing until the next time
You have no regard for my feelings, and again make me cry.....

Invisible Tears

Invisible tears trailing my cheeks
Camouflaged by a smile, both transparent and sleek
Proclaiming to be fine while masking silent cries
When deep down inside, I'm imprisoned in my mind
Pride too strong to admit pain or weakness
Resulting in barricaded emotions
Many nights long and sleepless
Carrying the weight of uncharted decisions
With no safety net or airbags to brace unexpected collisions
Determined to maintain, with spells of haziness
Driving in reverse, in and out of lanes
Knees sore from praying
Clocks broke from waiting
Toying with the consideration of the easier temptations
Not wanting to give in because earning is more rewarding than taking
But when pushed against the wall
The right way isn't the only option debating
Trying not to dive in blindly
Treading in an ocean with visions of hope
Head barely above water
But determined to stay afloat

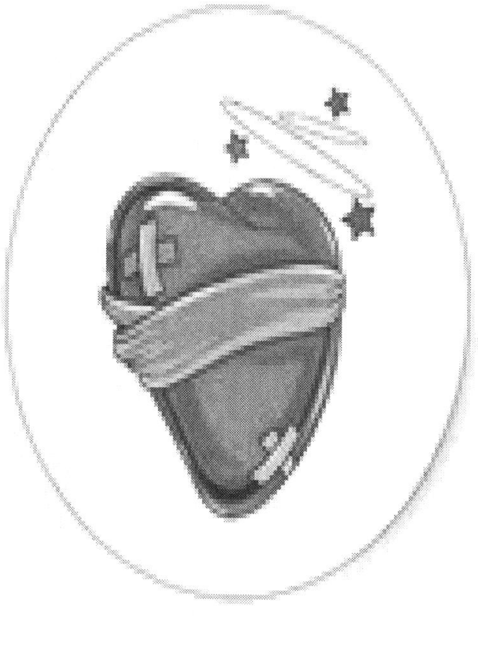

Passive Aggressive Heart

Diary entry;

Passive aggression of the heart
Validated by synthetic kisses
Persuading my mind that this is a perfect moment
Trying convincingly to ignore it for what it really is
Emotion for me… pleasure for you
Giving every part of me
Only receiving the demo version of you
Unfair trade off in exchange for diluted compliments
And lottery pick slots of your time
Everyone preaching to the choir
"It's not worth it" that I can do better
I deserve more
Instead I sacrifice myself defending you at war
Arguing that no pictures perfect
And yes to me he's worth it
I love and need this man
Tired of being alone
Misery only wants some company
Anyone who's been there before should understand
Besides I know that he loves me
He reassures me every time we make love
And even more right before he goes home to… her
But it's ok, because when he's with her

I know he's thinking about me
Gotta be, because I think about him
Every moment he's away
And ten times fold when he's not with me
On holidays
But it's ok
I don't mind having to share him
Something's better than nothing right
As long as he continues to break me off and warm my bed
And when she's away, I get to play wife
If only for one night
I mean really, what should I be bitter for
When we hooked up, I was with dude
And he said he had a wife
That things weren't good, just holding on for the child
Until the moment was right
And when all is said and done
It will be my time to shine
Sincerely his promise to me
Now three years' time
Sad story to some but a fairy tale of mines
He came close to leaving her a couple occasions
But his kids needed him
Once again convinced through heavy persuasion

I go with the flow because I understand
Wouldn't want him to stop playing daddy to my little man
He's all we got
And because I'm damaged
I'd rather accept a little and hope for a lot
Who has forever to wait for Mr. Right
I'd rather settle for Mr. Right now
Content with shadowing the spotlight
Blinded until the day I awake and realize
How much I've been living a lie
That I'm an extra in family guy's life
How he'll never intended to leave her
Or make me his wife
All the years I have wasted blinded by lies
When that day happens
I'll probably crumble and cry
Act totally confused like I don't know why
While he continues on and lives his life
Or I can end this cycle
Go with my first mind
Regain my confidence
Beauty divine
Want for more and not settle for less
Know that every struggle is a test
You must feel pain to understand happiness
That I deserve to be queen
I am a goddess in flesh

Painless

Who said love wasn't painless
Bleeding hearts don't lie
Builds you up to destroy you
Leave you asking why
I know I don't deserve this
But the pain means I'm alive
Can't escape from all the madness
So I bury it deep down inside
Why
Am I half the girl I used to be
Why
Am I slowly dying, please rescue me
I try
But every time I think I'm good
Good Lord I fall
All ten rounds I'm knock back down
Oh no, oh no

S.H.A.M.E O.N Y.O.U

S.elfish
H.ateful
A.ngry
M.ean
E.vil

O.nly thinking of yourself
N.ot always about you

Y.ou
O.ught to
U.nderstand by now

                Shame on you

Disappear

Disappear
Get out of my life
You've really pissed me off
You've earned your last strike
Disappear
I don't want you no mo'
The door is straight ahead
And it's time for you to go
Disappear
I'm tired of your games
The tie must be severed
You're shaming my name
A weight has been lifted
The end is here, make like magic
Out of thin air disappear

I'm Leaving

Twisted emotions and I don't know what to do
All the feelings we shared have somehow turned blue
As usual, things started good
Very special indeed
But something is missing
And it's something that I need
You told me you loved me and I said I loved you too
But the words I said were neither
Sincere, honest or true
The word love is now discouraging
And I'm not calling you the blame
But now the feelings in my heart aren't quite the same
To add on to all the confusion and strife
An old everlasting love has re-entered my life
Maybe I need a little time alone
To figure out where things went wrong
I'm not trying to be mean
But what I'm actually trying to say
Is that the love in my heart
Has somehow faded away

Love Was Here

Love what here, but now it's gone
But deep inside us, it will live on
We used to say it, it used to be true
Now it's a memory for both me and you
We used to dream that we would be together
For every tomorrow
Now our dream has turned to sorrow
Sometimes good relationships come to an end
But I hope and pray we will always be friends

You

You loved
I loved
You wanted trust
I gave you trust
You swore
I believed
You lied
I found out
You deceived
I never should have believed...
You would change

Voicemail ... Final Warning

I feel like I'm caught in your web of lies... The more and more I try to break free, the more you spin and throw at me... and silly me, I give in and surrender just like you knew I would... believing things would change and it would be all good...
Like always it temporarily gets better... just long enough for me to settle back down... get back into the usual flow of things... Then here we go again... Sad forecast... more bad weather! You're so predictable... I read through you like a letter.
Why do I continue to let you get to me like this??? You got me buggin'... steppin out of character... an emotional wreck... and now I'm pissed!!! Knowing you're insulting my intelligence, tryna play me for a fool... I keep trying to convince myself, naw that's not what it is... And that's the problem.... I keep making excuses for you... playing myself like a fool assisting you...
Every now and then I get pushed to the limit and gather the courage to put you out... Only for me to start missing you, believing you... then let you back in... Once Again! Telling me your sorry for the

Hundredth time... just like an old record that keeps skipping, repeating the same ole' sad lines.

Love can be vindictive... and whoever said it doesn't hurt told a bold face lie...

Bad love can make you foolish and jeopardize your pride...

Tell me why do you lie... why do you put me down, make me sad then watch me cry??? Know this... Karma is a bitch!!! It always manages to come back around and bite you where you sit... aint that a trip!!! So the next time you're out late, not answering the phone when I call... doing God knows what with who... lying, pretending you're playing ball... When it all boils down and the truth is revealed... You will be the one to fall!!!

I know my worth, and if you don't, I hope you figure it out soon... before the storm that we are enduring upgrades to a typhoon... I know you heard me say this time and time before.... but at last I'm growing stronger, and I simply can't take your misuse any longer!!! You need to learn how to appreciate me, and give me the same respect I give you... because if you don't, there is always another more than willing too!!! You can't stand to hear that, and you can get mad all you want... I'm just simply stating the facts...

How would you like it if the roles were reversed and I left you home alone crying... filling your head with

The same b.s you feed me... while your hearts slowly dying... Now that I mention it, the thought of that isn't sounding too bad...
I'm a woman scorned... love has drained me... made me bitter, and now I'm mad... Not just mad at you but disappointed in myself because I allowed you to break me down... and that's not good for my mental health... With all that being said, this is my final warning... My very last plea... I'm regaining the strength of my heart... I'm looking out for me!!! I refuse to let you put me through this anymore... The next time I'm permanently closing and locking my door... Once it's locked, it's locked forever... The tie that bonds us will be severed...I know all this sounds bad but truth hurts.... These changes will and must happen... It's time for you to be held accountable for all your actions... I love you... yes I do... but I'm tired of all the hurt and pain... It's making me lose focus... driving me insane...

There's a very thin line between love and hate... I just hope you realize all of this before it's too late...

This is my final warning!!!

Infinite Thoughts of Motivation and Inspiration

Motivation Equals Determination

Dedication and determination
Ignites my motivation to chase, challenge
And accomplish the goals I have set forth
Eager yet humble
Shall I be on my quest for success
Never once taking my feet off stable grounds
Never falling short of giving thanks and praise
To the almighty who strengthens me
And breathes life into my entire existence
Through all this I will be jubilant
I will proudly be able to bask in the gratification
Of my success and accomplishments that
I am destined and determined to obtain

Sweet Merlot

A crescent smile on her face to camouflage the bitter sweet disdain in her heart
Drowning her sorrows with the last remnants of the wine she poured from a glass that was once full
As she raises the glass she can't help but feel empathy for the bottle that now sits empty at her side
Like that of the bottle she too feels empty
Void of the contents that once overflowed abundantly
Until drained and relinquished of its sweet nectar and natural essence
With an ever so gentle hand she traces the rim of the glass
And with a gentle mind she retraces the memories and moments that once intoxicated her, like the merlot that now flowed freely through her body
Lost in thought and engulfed by her elixir
With one deep sigh she devours the remains of her glass

With a careen hand, she tries to place it on the table,
but alike her emotions... it slipped from her grasp and
shattered
With that precise moment being frozen in time, she
couldn't help but notice a single drop trickling
timelessly down the
Leg of the table... Symbolic to the single tear now
rolling down her blushed cheek
As she knelt down and began picking up the pieces of
glass... it was then at that precise moment that she
decided... she decided that like the glass she too
would begin to start picking up the pieces of her life,
and all the things she thought she lost grip of
No longer would she allow herself, anything, or
anyone to make her feel broken
Never again would she allow herself to feel empty,
drained, relinquished of her essence... her passion...
because there was a flame that still burned dimly
deep down inside of her
So for each piece she picked up, she dedicated it to
each thing about her life she wanted to pick up and
repair
First were her spirit and her pride... because if she
allowed herself to continue feeling down, how could
she ever begin to start picking up the pieces

How could things change for the better
One by one... her heart... her mind... her body... her happiness... her smile... her dignity... that one thing that made her, her
Now that all this things, these shattered pieces, were now in the palms of her hands
She claimed them to be uplifted
This would be the start of her life as new
No more sorrow... no more pain... no more tears, or hurt
All these things would cease to exist
She was now seeing in a different light
Self-proclaimed
She would become a better her
Only she would have control of her life and what would become of it
Sweet Merlot... both bitter and sweet
A better her

新開始

Lost and Found

I'm calling out to you
Where are you hiding
You been gone long from me
Soul searching with no findings
I'm lost and confused
Staring at a reflection
I don't know you
Where did you go, why did you leave
Did I disappoint you, force us to retreat
Still holding on because I know your there
I'm going to find you
Much damage to repair
I need you here
Come back to me
Never will I neglect you
I'm making time for me
Losing oneself isn't hard at all
Holding strong and mending broken pieces
Is the biggest struggle of them all
But I know where I went wrong
Self-neglect
I lost focus

Gave all that I could
Until I was empty, cold and hopeless
Watching the person I used to be
Run away from home
Understanding why you left
Solitaire confinement of the mind
Auto pilot steering me through time
Past shattered dreams empty promises and broken hearts
It's time for me to take control of the wheel
Chance at a brand new start
Regaining strength with a new sense of direction
Prepared to move forward with no hesitation
Returning to the person I used to be
May be a challenge both bitter sweet
But in the end it's worth finding me

Confident

So desirable and inspirable
Memorable respectable and extremely beautiful
Intellectual who is oh so loveable, unforgettable and
Delectable
Untouchable usually unpredictable
And enviable to those less suitable
For all not to love her is inevitable

Beautiful woman

Beautiful women stand up we hold the key to the future of the nation through us we breathe life. We are the original mothers of the human creation understand who you are and the power we possess let's stop identifying by our looks our asses and our breast. Always looking for the man with the fat pockets and fancy cars and shoes instead cherish your body your intellect guard your heart protect your jewels. Don't settle for less demanding your respect never abandon your principles for anyone empower yourself never self-neglect. Quit accommodating or demeaning yourselves at the expense of others. Find a King that will honor love and respect who you are instead of chasing disrespectful, unappreciative and neglectful lovers. It's not until you can define yourself, before you can identify with another. Stand up and claim what is rightfully yours. Be the foundation for your family be the backbone for your children. Infuse values in your beautiful little princess daughters. We need to stop objectifying and demeaning each other. Stop fighting with one another. We need to stand tall educate and empower.

Unite with our fellow sisters and brothers. Don't fall victim to the system that was set up to destroy our people and make us fail. Let us show that we have a voice and won't be made silent. We have to live outside our so-called designated boxes and programming. Let's give the manipulators hell. Independently we must come together to uplift and strengthen our nation as a whole. Dig deep into our roots and heritage. Stand up and reclaim our home and our gold. We can do it all we have to do is put forth the effort and try. We can't forget what our ancestors went through and fought for. We can't let our lineage die. Beautiful women it's time to stop dreaming because it's time to wake up and start living.

Infinite Thoughts

Thinking Outside the Box

Beware

This here is shaken not stirred
And can easily dismantle
I might deliver a dose that's more than you can handle
Viewer discretion
Last chance to change the channel
You can't control the urge to bite
If you un muzzle an animal
You knew what it would be
If you stepped in my yard
The sign on the fence said beware of dog

Propaganda

Quit believing all the bullshit they keep feeding your head
All this hypocrisy a.k.a our democracy is dead
People are to blind to see, still caught up in fantasy land
While they keep us nearer
Watching through their two way mirrors
The hell with privacy
Try to run and they'll find and seek
Proclaiming freedom while a tight leash has you bleeding
Caged and bounded in a land our people founded
Learn your history
New age slave by their trade
Revolt and fight up out the grave
Whether you win or lose
The choice is yours to choose
Push Love instead of hatred
Drop the pills
Step out of the matrix
Stop being simple minded
Think for yourself don't be blindly guided
If knowledge is power, seek and devour it
Time to get your head out the clouds
Conquer your own demons and cast them out

The walls will come crashing down
If we break free and knock them down
Uplift, Help and Encourage
Working together we are bound to move forward
Don't be bullied by a crooked system
If we shout loud enough they will have to listen
Together united hand in hand
We can't be defeated if we firmly stand
The time is now for us to stand and say we are tired
of being lied to
We are tired of being demeaned and undervalued
We come from Greatness, therefore we are Greatness
We need to move forward and release the forces
within
Awaken our conscious minds
The truth is out there and it's yours to find
Hotep

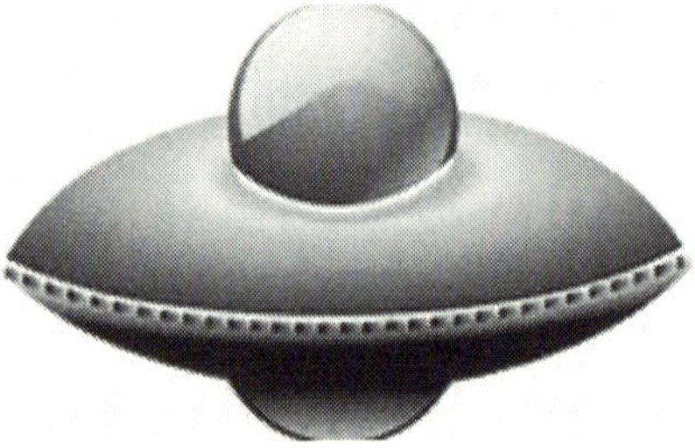

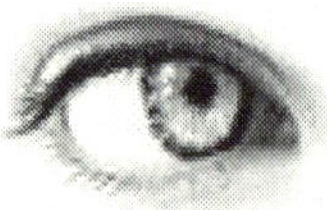

Eye to the Sky

Star gazing late night through binocular lenses
Fixated on a star flickering like a disco ball in HD vision
Adjusted focus and a couple blinks of the eye
Wondering am I tripping because twinkle twinkle is definitely
Lightning up the midnight skies
A couple of flickers and one bright flash
I guess the star was a shooter because it shot off fast
Confused and dazed, do I make a wish
Reality shot back in, shooting stars don't exist
Fairy tale lies they told us to divert us from the big pic
Like there's no life on mars and ufo's don't exist
Go check the Sumerian text
They show the god's hovering and descending from our heavenly skies
Symbolic to the chariots and angels when heaven arrives
You can choose to believe the propaganda they feed you
Or manifest the power of your own mind
Pray to God as yourself
Stay rooted to the ground and your eyes to the sky

The Matrix

Trapped and enslaved within the matrix of our minds
Reality misconstrued
Receiving our daily dose of programming via Xbox, flat screen,
Or YouTube... better yet the news
Selective broadcasting promoting fear, sex, lies and deception
F.D.A legally selling drug for depression
Fixed elections, designated Hitler lizard like politicians
Syndicate mental slavery with repetition
Black mom arrested for enrolling her kid I a prominent School district
They fined her, embarrassed her,
Claimed she was out her jurisdiction
All she wanted was better education
But she's an urban girl living in a suburban world
So it's back to segregation
When fighting for a cause, it's hard to stay peaceful
Criticized for having melanin,
Not treated as equals
Forgetting first and foremost that we are all God's people

Release the veil, invoke higher levels of consciousness
Conquer beyond their boundaries
Increase your intelligence
Discover and uncover the history of our true past, and relevance
Where the mind leads, the body will follow
Devote life to positive thinking
Watch it manifest ridding you of greed, hate fear and sorrow
Collectively raise the frequencies
Good vibrations create better tomorrows
We are all vessels of light in physical form
Spiritually connected offspring's of divine power
Dynamic capabilities reign down from far beyond meteor showers
The true nature of who we are and the abilities we possess
10 dormant strands of DNA awaiting activation
God like qualities ready to manifest
The time is now to get the world back to positive vibrations
Spiritually reconnect with the multi and heavenly dimensions
Spread peace, love and harmony
Through enlightenment comes ascension

Infinite Thoughts
Sincere Dedications

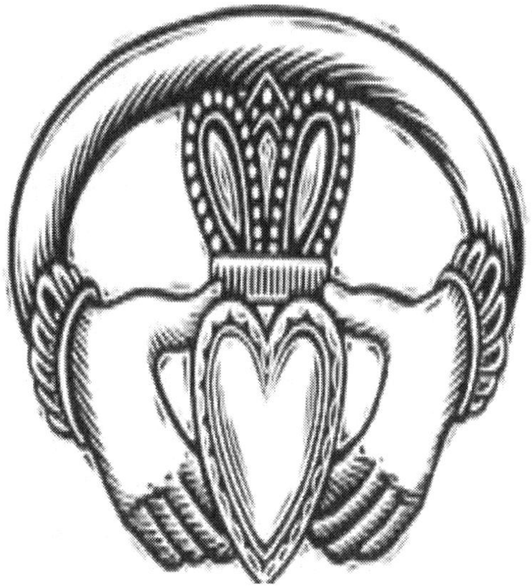

My King

Powerful is both the mind and creative thought
Knowing exactly what I wanted and needed
I thought you into my existence
And at my doorstep you appeared
An exact manifestation of the man of my dreams
A king in every essence
Confident yet humble
AmBitious and **worthy of his queen**
I embrace you
You represent love and life in my eyes
Both which you dynamically changed
Through your passion and sincerity
You redefined my views on love and happiness
Showing me true love
And that all I experienced before you
Were the pre requisites of life to prepare me for
The authentic experience of you
The epitome of a real man
A role model for his sons
A lover and provider to his wife
An example of a real man for his daughters
You are the backbone of our family
I vow to stand with you and never against you
Just as you vow to never put another before me

You always honor, respect and protect what's yours
My king
Proud to wear his ring as a badge of honor
I am your queen
Mind, body and soul
His only pleasure
Never another
You have brought my dreams to reality
And together we will create our own
I am grateful for you
I am proud to be a compliment of your life
Proud to be your wife
Never have I imagined finding a love so pure
I overstand that we are twin flame
My king
I will love you in flesh with every breath
And forever in spirit
My king sincerely your queen

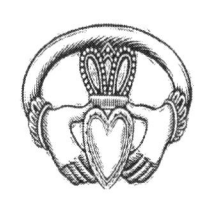

Mother

Divine beauty
Shinning her light from within
A true matriarch of family
Role model, mother and friend
More than a woman
A warrior and queen
Who's strength is enduring
Intelligent and keen
Her love has never wavered
Holding her children near to her heart
Providing us light
When we're stuck in the dark
Gentle when needed
But always remaining strong
Instilling good values
Teaching us right from wrong
Having patience when we ignore your advice

Not saying I told you so
When you turn out to be right
Feeding us the nourishment s
Of all the knowledge she knows
Preparing us for life
And allowing us to grow
Always understanding
Inspirational in every way
The purest form of love she gives
From cradle to the grave
A bond that could never be severed
A love which never ends
God's gift to this world
My mother, my role model, my friend

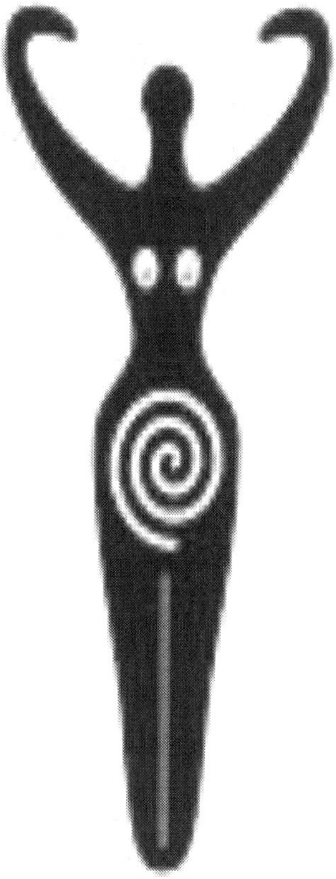

Creation Within

Creation of love
Created by love
Incarnation of spirit
Dwelling within the godly womb
Which I breed life
Intertwined
We live and grow as one
Two heartbeats beating simultaneously
Yours and mines
As I nourish and develop you nine months' time
I feel you grow
I feel your flutters
Sharing a divine connection between child and mother
Projecting a glow as my belly rounds
Enduring many changes as the clock winds down
Awaiting the sacred moment of giving birth
Your first breaths
Your first cry
Miraculous is the creation and producing of life

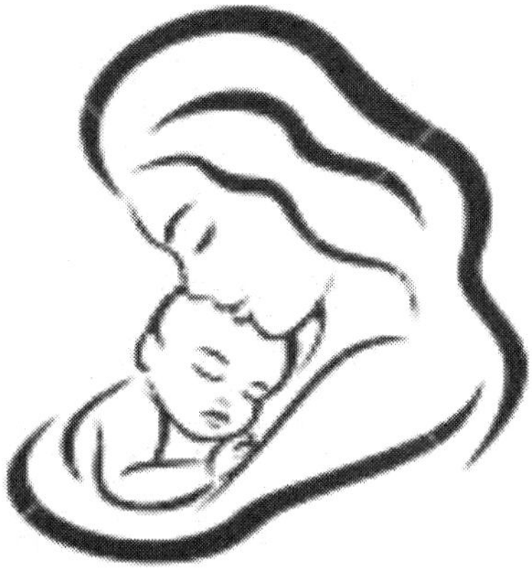

My Child

You are my life
You are my motivation
You are my encouragement
You are my determination
You are my joy
You are my thoughts
You are my mirror
You are the beat of my heart
You are my happiness
You are my reason to smile
You are the blessings given to me
You are my children
You are my child

Anxiously Expecting

Anxiously expecting
And anticipating the first moment
I hold you in my arms
The excitement of hearing your first cry
The familiarity I'll feel when I look into your eyes
Joy filled will be your father and I
Of our creation of love
Our child divine
Expecting the blessing of a baby girl
Family of love
awaiting to welcome you to the world

Found

I was once a person who could never be found
Soul lost... feelings buried... emotions deep underground
Inside I cried
My tears soaked the ground
Flooding the secrets I hold... but the never seem to drown
Then you came around
Now I see myself for the person I am
Once stuck in a traffic jam
You gave me a helping hand and showed me how to love Again
We are soul mates
Feelings are deep and too strong to hide
Happy I found the love I dreamed of
Is now by my side

OBVIAZ

OBVIAZ

Ovlina

O is for the **O**pportunity for blessing me with your presence
V is for the **V**arious ways I feel when wrapped in your arms
L is for the **L**oyalty and love I have for you
I is for the **I**mpact you have made in my life
N is for **N**ever judging me no matter how wrong or right
A is for **A**lways loving me and being my inspiration

OBVIAZ

Family Tree in Concrete

There is a beautiful oak tree standing tall as the sky
Leaves barely full but branches spread far and wide
At one point very full
Till winds blew strong
Shaking off seeds
to start a life of their own
But the tree was slowly dying
Not healthy as it could be
The tree was not grounded in earth
But rooted in concrete
Not the greatest of foundations
For it to grow joyously
Instead entangled in stone
Disrupting natural harmony
But the tree was determined
Grew stronger roots and crumbled the ground
With the help of wind, and a passing storm
new soil covered them
Creating a mound
All natural elements to restart
Both Healthy and new
With hopes to strengthen the foundation
And continue to bloom

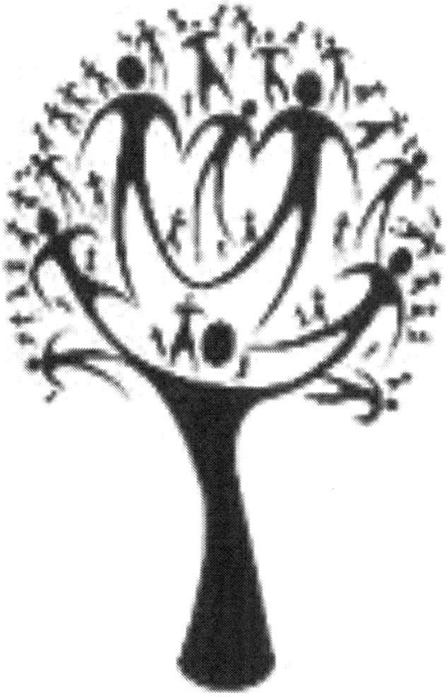

Devil in Disguise

Devil in disguise
Master at your game
Puppet master manipulating
The strings of my brain
Twisted with deception
Rotten to the core
You had a thirst for my pain
Secretly lusting for more
Flames in your eyes
Evil in your heart
You were wicked enough to really consider
"Till Death Do Us Part"
You had an accomplice
The apple doesn't fall to far from the tree
You inherited your venom
Genetically
Tried to control me
With your wicked charm

The veil has been lifted
I see you all for who you really are
No longer a victim
I escaped being your prey
I broke free of your shackles
You no longer stand in my way
I've regained my strength
Standing tall on my own two feet
I proclaim with the deepest passion
That you will never again have a hold over me
I don't hate you
I pity and appreciate you
I even pray for your souls
I've learned valuable life lessons because of you
I overcame your torment, and regained control
I can sincerely say for the first time...
I am finally free
The devils disguise has been revealed
I wish only the best for you and that your souls find peace

Last words, final thoughts

You didn't win...

Good always prevails...

In the darkest room

The smallest light has the Power to brighten and Enlighten

Watch me glow!

OBVIAZ

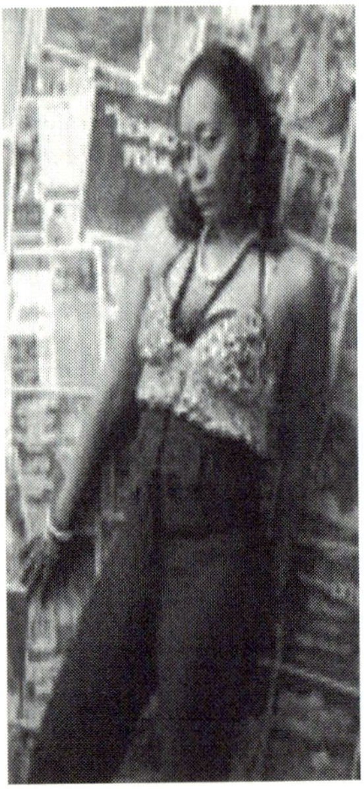

About the Author

Ovlina Lewis is a poet, author, song writer, healer, Reiki practitioner, lover of life and friend. Ovlina is the proud mother and queen of three beautiful princess daughters and a handsome prince son. She finds inspirations for her writings through the many experiences of life, emotions and everyday situations through her eyes and the eyes of others. Through her work she wishes to connect to the hearts and spirit of her readers with hopes of inspiring or providing new ways of viewing life and all it has to bring. So toast to having the glass half full as opposed to half empty.

To my king Anthony, my children Jayland, Laniah, Olivia, Athena and my loving family, you are my inspiration and motivation.

I love you

thinking THE BOX

Made in the USA
Charleston, SC
14 April 2013